DATE D

DISCOVERING
CAREERS FOR YOUR FUTURE

computers

Ferguson Publishing Company
Chicago, Illinois

Carol Yehling
Editor

Beth Adler, Herman Adler Design Group
Cover design

Carol Yehling
Interior design

Bonnie Needham
Proofreader

Library of Congress Cataloging-in-Publication Data

Discovering careers for your future. Computers.
    p. cm.
  ISBN 0-89434-389-0
1. Computer science—Vocational guidance I. Title: Computers. II. Ferguson Publishing Company.

QA76.25 .D57 2001
004'.023'73—dc21

                                                                    00-049519

Published and distributed by
Ferguson Publishing Company
200 West Jackson Boulevard, 7th Floor
Chicago, Illinois 60606
800-306-9941
www.fergpubco.com

Printed in the United States of America
Y-4

Table of Contents

Introduction

You may not have decided yet what you want to be in the future. And you don't have to decide right away. You do know that right now you are interested in computers. Do any of the statements below describe you? If so, you may want to begin thinking about what a career in computers might mean for you.

___My favorite school assignments are the ones I do on the computer.

___I spend a lot of time surfing the Internet.

___I use email to communicate with my friends.

___I enjoy teaching others how to use computers.

___I am good at computer games.

___I designed my own Web site.

___I like to take things apart and put them back together.

___I am interested in computer languages.

___I would like to learn more about how to build computers.

___I know how to do minor repairs on my computer.

___I belong to a computer club.

___I am interested in writing new software programs.

___I keep up with all the latest computer technology.

Discovering Careers for Your Future: Computers is a book about careers in computers, from computer-aided design technicians to webmasters. Just about any career will require you to have some computer knowledge. Technology changes so quickly that computer specialists will be in constant demand for a long time. Computers offer opportunities in developing that technology, writing new programs, exploring Internet possibilities, and managing the day-to-day operations of computers.

This book describes many possibilities for future careers that focus on computers. Read through it and see how the different careers are connected. For example, if you are interested in software, you will want to read the chapters on Computer and Video Game Designers, Computer Programmers, Computer Trainers, Graphics Programmers, Software Designers, and Software Engineers. If you are interested in the Internet, you will want to read the chapters on Internet Computer Security Specialists, Content Developers, and Webmasters. Go ahead and explore!

What do computer specialists do?

The first section of each chapter begins with a heading such as "What Computer Network Administrators Do" or "What Hardware Engineers Do." It tells what it's like to work at this job. It describes typical responsibilities and assignments. You will find out about working conditions. Which computer specialists work alone and which ones work on teams? Do they work in one location or do they travel to various locations? This section answers all these questions.

How do I become a computer specialist?

The section called "Education and Training" tells you what schooling you need for employment in each job—a high school diploma, training at a junior college, a college degree, or more. It also talks about on-the-job training that you could expect to receive after you're hired, and whether or not you must complete an apprenticeship program.

How much do computer specialists earn?

The "Earnings" section gives the average salary figures for the job described in the chapter. These figures give you a general idea of how much money people with this job can make. Keep in mind that many people really earn more or less than the amounts given here because actual salaries depend on many different things, such as the size of the company, the location of the company, and the amount of education, training, and experience you have. Generally, but not always, bigger companies located in major cities pay more than smaller ones in smaller cities and towns, and people with more education, training, and experience earn more. Also remember that these figures are current averages. They will probably be different by the time you are ready to enter the workforce.

What will the future be like for computer specialists?

The "Outlook" section discusses the employment outlook for the career: whether the total number of people employed in this career will increase or decrease in the coming years and whether jobs in this field will be easy or hard to find. These predictions are based on economic conditions, the size and makeup of the population, foreign competition, and new technology. Terms such as "faster than the average," "about as fast as the average," and "slower than the average," are terms used by the U.S. Department of Labor to describe job growth predicted by government data.

Keep in mind that these predictions are general statements. No one knows for sure what the future will be like. Also remember that the employment outlook is a general statement about an industry and does not necessarily apply to everyone. A determined and talented person may be able to find a job in an industry or career with the worst kind of outlook. And a person without ambition and the proper training will find it difficult to find a job in even a booming industry or career field.

Where can I find more information?

Each chapter includes a sidebar called "For More Info." It lists organizations that you can contact to find out more about the field and careers in the field. You will find names, addresses, phone numbers, and Web sites.

Extras

Every chapter has a few extras. There are photos that show artists in action. There are sidebars and notes on ways to explore the field, related jobs, fun facts, profiles of people in the field, or lists of Web sites and books that might be helpful. At the end of the book you will find a glossary and an index. The glossary gives brief definitions of words that relate to education, career training, or employment that you may be unfamiliar with. The index includes all the job titles mentioned in the book. It is followed by a list of general computer Web sites.

It's not too soon to think about your future. We hope you discover several possible career choices. Happy hunting!

Computer Aided Design Technicians

What Computer Aided Design Technicians Do

Computer aided design technicians, also called *CAD technicians,* use computers to design, improve, or make products and the machines that manufacture them. CAD usually stands for computer aided design, but it can also mean computer aided drafting. CAD technicians work in all parts of the manufacturing process. They assist engineers and designers, who are experts in applying computer technology in industrial design and manufacturing.

CAD technicians who help design and develop new products have both drafting and computer skills. They usually work at specially designed computer workstations. They use computer programs to change data files into diagrams and drawings of a product. The video screen acts as an electronic drawing board. CAD engineers or designers give CAD technicians instructions for changes to make in diagrams and drawings. They can either

IBM

type the changes into the computer or touch a stylus or light pen on the screen.

After they make the changes, technicians display the new diagrams or drawings. They repeat the process until a final design is approved. CAD technicians not only work on product designs, but also make detailed drawings of each part to be manufactured, as well as the tools that will assemble and join the parts.

CAD technicians work in architecture, electronics, and the manufacturing of automobiles, aircraft, computers, machinery, and missiles.

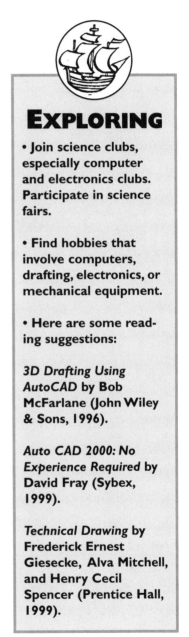

EXPLORING

• Join science clubs, especially computer and electronics clubs. Participate in science fairs.

• Find hobbies that involve computers, drafting, electronics, or mechanical equipment.

• Here are some reading suggestions:

3D Drafting Using AutoCAD by Bob McFarlane (John Wiley & Sons, 1996).

Auto CAD 2000: No Experience Required by David Fray (Sybex, 1999).

Technical Drawing by Frederick Ernest Giesecke, Alva Mitchell, and Henry Cecil Spencer (Prentice Hall, 1999).

DRAFTING: THEN AND NOW

A lot has changed for drafters and technicians in the last 30 years.

THEN
- Computers were large, sometimes filling entire rooms.
- Drafting was done on a drafting board, using T-squares, triangles, and pen and ink.
- If plans needed to be changed, a drafter would have to draw an entire new design.
- Drafting plans were sent using mailing tubes and large sheets of paper.

NOW
- Computers are smaller, faster, and more efficient.
- Drafting is done at a CAD workstation.
- If a plan needs changes, edits to the original can be quickly made on screen.
- Drafting plans can be sent easily through the Internet.

Education and Training

CAD technicians must have at least a high school diploma. Most go on to complete a two-year program at a technical school. Two-year programs include courses in basic drafting, machine drawing, architecture, civil drafting (with an emphasis on highways), piping, electrical, electrical instrumentation, and plumbing. Most training programs also include courses in data processing and computer programming, systems, and equipment.

Earnings

Apprentice CAD technicians can earn about $17,300 per year. Experienced technicians earn about $33,400 a year and the most experienced earn around $49,500. Some technicians with special skills, extensive experience, or additional responsibilities can earn even more. The U.S. Department of Labor reports that salaries for drafters ranged from $21,200 to $52,000 a year in 1998.

Outlook

Many companies will need to increase productivity in design and manufacturing activities. CAD technology provides some of the best opportunities to improve that productivity. Experts estimate there will be as many as a million jobs available in the next few years. The U.S. Department of Labor, however, predicts that the employment outlook for drafters will grow more slowly than the average for all other occupations through 2008.

Auto manufacturing and construction industries are affected by the economy, so any economic downturn could affect jobs for CAD technicians. The best opportunities will be for

FOR MORE INFO

For more information about the career of computer aided design technician, contact:
American Design and Drafting Association
PO Box 11937
Columbia, SC 29211
803-771-0008
http://www.adda.org

Institute of Electrical and Electronics Engineers
1828 L Street, NW, Suite 1202
Washington, DC 20036-5104
202-785-0017
http://www.ieee.org/usab

Society of Manufacturing Engineers
One SME Drive
Dearborn, MI 48121
800-733-4763
http://www.sme.org

drafters and technicians who keep up with new technology and continue to learn, both in school and on the job.

RELATED JOBS

Drafters
Graphic Designers
Graphics Programmers

Computer and Electronics Sales Representatives

The Art of Sales

Tell it like it is. Don't confuse the customer with computer lingo and don't be dishonest.

Sell customers what they want, not what you think they need. For example, don't try to sell a PC to someone who wants a Macintosh, or vice versa.

Know the products you are selling.

Listen to your customers. Find out what their software needs are first before you determine the choices of hardware and peripherals.

Use humor to put your customers at ease. Make sure they know that there is no such thing as a stupid question.

What Computer and Electronics Sales Representatives Do

Computer and electronics sales representatives sell computer electronics equipment to customers and businesses of all sizes. Sometimes they also install systems, provide maintenance, or train the client's staff. Sales representatives that work for retail stores deal with consumers. Representatives that specialize in a particular piece of hardware, certain software program, or electronic component may do business with banks, insurance companies, or accounting firms, among others.

The first step in the selling process is client consultation. Sales representatives find out the client's current and future technological needs. Often, customers do not have expertise in computer or electronics technology, so the rep must explain and translate complicated computer tech-talk, as well as answer numerous questions. Reps advise customers which system, peripherals, or software will best meet their needs and fit within their price range. When the customer makes a final choice, reps handle paperwork, including financing plans, servicing agreements, and payment. They assemble the order or arrange for delivery if requested.

To keep up with technological advances, sales representatives must attend training sessions or continuing education classes. Reps who specialize must also keep up with changing needs of particular industries, such as insurance or banking.

Education and Training

Classes in speech and writing help you learn how to present a product to large groups of people. Computer science and electronics classes will give you a basic overview of the field. General business and math classes are also helpful.

Computer sales representatives who specialize in a specific industry, such as health care or banking, need training in current issues of that field. Such training is available through special work training

EXPLORING

• Join computer clubs organized by your school or community center.

• Read computer magazines and newsletters, as well as online bulletin boards.

• Keep up with the latest computer equipment, including hardware, software, printers, pointing devices, scanners, and digital cameras.

seminars, adult education classes, or courses at a technical school. Many companies require their sales staff to complete a company training program where they learn the technologies and work tools they need.

Computer and electronics sales reps need to know a little about a large number of products. They also need to know about the computer and electronics industries as a whole so they can better advise their customers. Many manufacturers provide product introductions and hands-on training sessions specifically to help salespeople sell their products.

Earnings

Electronics and computer sales representatives working in retail start out earning an hourly wage—usually minimum wage, or $5.15 an hour. In addition, they earn commissions, or a percentage of sales they make. According to the Department of Labor, earnings of sales representatives, except retail, were $36,500, including commission, in 1998. Top salaries were more than $83,000.

SALES FIGURES 2000

During 2000 there were higher sales in electronics products than computer-related products. According to NPD INTELECT® Market Tracking, the fastest growing technology categories in 2000 were:

- Home networking products (up 300 percent)

- Personal digital assistants (up 163 percent)

- DVD players (up 108.3 percent)

- CD recordable drives (up 83.2 percent)

Notebooks and printers were up 3 percent and 6 percent respectively. The sales of inkjet cartridges and laser toner, increased 22 percent, but desktop purchases decreased 16 percent. Sales of monitors, printers, and laptops also decreased slightly.

According to a recent WetFeet.com industry study, sales associates who specialize in hardware components earned between $45,000 and $60,000 a year including commissions. Experienced account representatives in the computer/information field earned yearly salaries of about $52,000. Sales managers earned about $75,000 and marketing managers earned $104,125 a year.

Outlook

Employment opportunities should grow about as fast as the average for computer and electronics retail sales careers through the year 2008. There will be employment opportunities with computer specialty stores or consulting companies that deal directly with businesses and their corporate computer and application needs.

Working in sales can teach you a lot about computers very quickly and give you opportunities to move into other computer careers.

FOR MORE INFO

National Association of Retail Dealers of America
10 East 22nd Street
Lombard, IL 60148-4915
630-953-8950
http://www.narda.com

Association for Computing Machinery
1515 Broadway
New York, NY 10036-5701
212-869-7440
http://www.acm.org

The Electronics Representatives Association
444 North Michigan Avenue, Suite 1960
Chicago, IL 60611
312-527-3050
http://www.era.org

RELATED JOBS

Customer Service Representatives
Printing Sales Representatives
Real Estate Agents and Brokers
Retail Sales Workers
Sales Representatives
Services Sales Representatives
Wireless Sales Workers

Computer and Office Machine Technicians

What Computer and Office Machine Technicians Do

Computers and office machines are incredibly complex. Highly skilled electronics technicians keep computers and office machines operating properly and efficiently. *Computer and office machine technicians* service, install, calibrate, operate, maintain, and repair computers, peripherals, and other office machines.

Computer and office machine technicians work for computer manufacturers, large corporations, or repair shops. Technicians who work for manufacturers learn how their company's products work and how to repair them when they break. Sometimes, technicians are employed by computer manufacturers at a customer's workplace, where they help plan and install new computer systems. They also perform regular maintenance to make sure the equipment continues to operate properly. If the equipment breaks down, technicians work together with the customers to fix it.

Some technicians work in the maintenance or service departments of large corporations. They work with many different types of machines, both mechanical and electronic.

Some computer and office machine technicians work for companies or repair shops that specialize in providing maintenance services to computer and office machine users. When equipment breaks down or needs regular maintenance, technicians are sent to the customers' offices to provide the necessary services.

Education and Training

Because computers and office machines are such complex electronic devices, the technicians who work on them must have excellent engineering, electrical, and mechanical skills. Knowledge of computer programming is also important. Technicians must be able to follow written and spoken instructions and be able to communicate well.

EXPLORING

• Join one of the many computer user groups on the Internet.

• Participate in school computer or shop clubs.

• Try building your own computer or repairing discarded computer equipment.

RELATED JOBS

Computer and Electronics Sales Representatives

Electronics Engineering Technicians

Electronics Service Technicians

Hardware Engineers

Wireless Sales Workers

The best way to prepare for this career is to attend a special two-year program after high school. These programs are offered by technical institutes and some community colleges.

A variety of certification programs are available from the International Society of Certified Electronics Technicians, the Institute for Certification of Computing Professionals, the Association of Energy Engineers, and the Electronics Technicians Association and Satellite Dealers Association, among other organizations. You can be certified in fields such as computer, industrial, or electronic equipment.

OFFICE MACHINES OVER TIME

The history of office machines goes back to ancient Babylonia and the invention of the abacus, a manual calculating device. The abacus is considered an ancestor of the computer.

In the 17th century, French mathematician and philosopher Blaise Pascal developed the first digital machine that could perform addition and subtraction. American inventor William Burroughs developed the first truly practical adding machine in 1894.

The typewriter's history dates to the 19th century, although at this time many cumbersome typing machines were as big as pianos, and others resembled clocks. By the 1870s the Remington Company was producing much more practical machines. Thomas Edison invented the first electrically operated typewriter in 1872, and by the 1930s, such machines were being used in offices.

The computer is the most recently engineered office machine. The first experimental versions of modern computers were built during the 1940s. Technical improvements made during the 1950s led to the first commercial computers. By the late 1950s and early 1960s, the transistor was developed and in the late 1960s integrated circuitry led to the development of minicomputers. In the early 1970s, the microprocessor became the heart of the modern computer. The development of the silicon chip opened up many new uses for computers.

Earnings

According to the U.S. Department of Labor, in 1998, service technicians who specialized in communications and industrial electronic equipment earned average annual salaries of $31,300. Computer equipment service technicians earned an average of $30,264 a year. Technicians with extensive work experience and certification earn more.

Outlook

According to the U.S. Department of Labor, employment opportunities for computer and office machine technicians are expected to grow about 40 percent faster than the average for all other occupations through 2008. Demand for service technicians who specialize in commercial and industrial electronic equipment is expected to grow about 12 percent. Demand for service technicians who specialize in office equipment repair is expected to grow only as fast as the average.

FOR MORE INFO

For industry information or details on their certification program, contact:
International Society of Certified Electronics Technicians
2708 West Berry Street
Fort Worth, TX 76109-2356
817-921-9101
http://www.iscet.org

Contact ACM for information on internships, student membership, and the ACM magazine, Crossroads. ACM also offers a student Web site at http://www.acm.org/membership/student/.
Association for Computing Machinery
1515 Broadway, 17th Floor
New York, NY 10036-5701
212-869-7440
http://www.acm.org

For certification, career, and placement information, contact:
Electronics Technicians Association and Satellite Dealers Association
502 North Jackson
Greencastle, IN 46135
765-653-4301
http://www.eta-sda.com

Computer and Video Game Designers

Read All About It

***Dombrower's Art of Interactive Entertainment Design* by Eddie Dombrower (McGraw-Hill, 1998).** This book tells you what to do if you're interested in computer games and how to create a game design. The author discusses the main principles of game design and how to create game design documents.

***Game Developer's Marketplace: The Definitive Guide to Making It Big in the Interactive Game Industry* by Ben Sawyer, Alex Dunne, and Tor Berg (Coriolis Group Books, 1998).** This book is packed with information about what it takes to be a game designer. It tells you how to write a design document and basics of game design. It includes a CD-ROM and lists of books, conferences, software, and Web resources.

What Computer and Video Game Designers Do

Computer and video game designers create the games played on computer and television and in arcades. They think up new game ideas, including sound effects, characters, story lines, and graphics. Some designers work full-time for the companies that make the games. Others might work as freelancers, designing games in their own studios and then selling their ideas and programs to production companies.

Each game must have a story as well as graphics and sound that will entertain and challenge the players. A game begins with careful planning and preparation. Designers write scripts, sketch storyboards (frame-by-frame drawings of the game's events), decide how the characters and places should look, and make notes on sound effects and other features.

Designers use computer programs, or write their own programs to assemble text, art, and sound into a digital video. There is a long process of reviewing and trial-and-error to correct problems and smooth rough spots. Designers usually create a basic game and then design several levels of difficulty for beginning to advanced players. It takes from about six to 18 months to design a computer or video game.

Designing computer games often requires a whole team of workers, including programmers, artists, musicians, writers, and animators. Computer and video game designers have a unique combination of highly technical skills and vivid, creative imaginations.

Education and Training

If you want to be a computer and video game designer, you need to learn many different computer skills, including programming. Art, literature, and music classes can help you develop your creativity.

You don't necessarily need a college degree to be a game designer, but most companies prefer to hire those with a bachelor's degree. There are a few

EXPLORING

• Try to design easy games, or experiment with games that have an editor. Games like *Klik & Play, Empire,* and *Doom* allow you to modify them to create new circumstances.

• Write your own stories, puzzles, and games to work on your storytelling and problem-solving skills.

• Read magazines like *Computer Graphics World* (http://www.cgw.com) and *Game Developer* (http://www.gdmag.com). They have articles about digital video and other technical and design information.

schools that offer training programs specifically for designing computer games. The DigiPen Institute in Redmond, Washington, and the Laboratory for Recreational Computing in Denton, Texas, are two such schools. (See For More Info.) The International Game Developers Association (http://www.igda.org) has a list of universities and trade schools with courses and/or degree programs in gaming.

Earnings

Computer and video game designers earn between $30,000 and $75,000 per year. Earnings depend on how much experience you have, where you live, the size of the company you work for, and whether you earn bonuses and royalties

TYPES OF COMPUTER GAMES

3D games: Games that feature 3D environments and usually include action and shooting, such as *Doom*.

RPG: Role-playing games, such as *Dungeons and Dragons*, that require building a character.

Adventure: Games that are puzzle-based, such as the *King/Police/Space Quest* series or Lucas Arts' *Indiana Jones* games.

Edutainment: Games that combine educational elements with game elements, such as *Carmen Sandiego* and *Rescue the Scientists*.

Retro games: Games, such as *Atari* classics, that are recreated on a new platform.

Simulation: Games that put the player in a seemingly real situation, such as *Flight Simulator, F-15 Strike Eagle*, and *Comanche*.

Sports games: Strategy games based on soccer, football, tennis, baseball, and other sports.

God games: Games that allow the player to control outcomes, such as *Sim City, Sim Earth*, and *Populus*.

Shooters: Games in which the player shoots at targets, such as *Raptor* or *Space Invaders* and *Asteroids*.

Fighting games: Games that feature hand-to-hand combat, such as *Mortal Kombat, Virtual Fighter, Street Fighter*, and *One Must Fall*.

Platform games: Vertical-scrolling screen games, such as *Donkey Kong, Commander Keen, Jazz Jackrabbit*, and *Duke Nukem*.

(a percentage of profits from each game that is sold).

Outlook

The computer and video game industry is growing quickly, with more and more companies hiring skilled people at many levels. Because the industry is fairly new, it is difficult to estimate exactly how many people work as game designers. About 90,000 people work within the video game industry as a whole.

Game development is popular—it is estimated that 15 million people in the United States have grown up playing computer and video games and that this number could go beyond 100 million by the year 2010. Designers should find good opportunities for jobs in the next 10 years as companies try to keep up with the demand for new games.

FOR MORE INFO

This organization fosters information exchange and communication among professionals in the computer game and interactive development industry.
International Game Developers Association
http://www.igda.org

This institute offers a bachelor of science degree in Real Time Interactive Simulation.
DigiPen Institute of Technology
5001 150th Avenue, NE
Redmond, WA 98052
http://www.digipen.edu

This university lab trains students in game design and programming.
The Laboratory for Recreational Computing
University of North Texas
Department of Computer Science
PO Box 311366
Denton, TX 76203-1366
http://hercule.csci.unt.edu/larc/info.html

RELATED JOBS

Computer Programmers
Graphics Programmers
Software Designers
Toy and Game Designers
Toy Industry Workers

Computer Network Specialists

What Computer Network Specialists Do

A computer network is a system of computer hardware, such as computers, terminals, printers, modems, and other equipment, which is linked together electronically. Networks allow many users to share computer equipment and software at the same time. Networks also allow busy workers to share files, view each other's schedules, and send email.

Computer network specialists make sure computer networks run properly at all times. They install, maintain, update, and repair network equipment and files. They also help train people how to use the network. Sometimes, they help a company decide which computer system to buy and help change existing software to better meet the needs of the business.

Computer network administrators manage the network. They work with the files and directories on the network's central computer, called the server. The server holds important files, including software applications, databases, and electronic mail services, all of which must be updated regularly. Some networks have separate servers for specific operations, such as communications or printing or databases.

Network security specialists concentrate most of their efforts on making sure that the computer system is safe from tampering. Security is very important because most companies store confidential information on their computers. Network security specialists can tell when unauthorized changes are made in the files and who makes them. They report these problems and devise better ways to eliminate such errors in the future. For example, one important school database that must be protected by security specialists involves student grades; only authorized personnel have access to these files.

Data recovery operators set up emergency computer sites in case the main computers experience major problems. Business emergencies, for example, can be caused by natural catastrophes, such as power outages, floods, and earthquakes. Data recovery operators choose alternative locations, decide which hard-

EXPLORING

• Join computer clubs at school and community centers.

• Ask your school district officials about the possibility of working with the school system's network specialists for a day or longer. Parents' or friends' employers might also be a good place to find this type of opportunity. Volunteer at local charities that use computer networks in their offices. Since many charities have small budgets, they may offer more opportunities to gain experience with some of the simpler networking tasks.

• Experiment by creating networks with your own computer, those of your friends, and any printers, modems, fax machines, or other peripherals.

ware and software should be stored there, and designate how often files should be backed up.

Education and Training

Classes in mathematics, science, and computers help you prepare for this career. All computer network specialists have bachelor's degrees in computer science or computer engineering. Many also earn official certification from a commercial educational center. The certification process is difficult and

MY LIFE AS A NETWORK ADMINISTRATOR

Dan Creedon of Nesbitt Burns Securities, talks about working in the networking industry:

"My primary duty is to protect my company's data on a Windows NT network. I make sure that employees have access to the data they need, and do not have access to information that they do not need. I protect the system from any kind of failure or disaster that might destroy or otherwise make data unavailable. I also perform system upgrades.

"Like many people in this field who started out right when the explosion of computer technology occurred, I worked in an office where I was the 'power user.' I was the person everyone came to with their questions. That led me to start learning more on my own, and then eventually to take a course in networking with Novell Netware. After that, I took a job with a small consulting firm as a Netware consultant. I was then placed at a company that used Netware and was getting ready to upgrade to Windows NT networks.

"One of the best parts of my job is that I work independently and on a fairly flexible schedule. Of course, that means that sometimes I must work after hours or on weekends, but that also allows me to schedule an extra personal day once in a while. Probably the worst part of my job is when I have to work with a nontechnical manager who doesn't understand that while some things might appear simple to him, they are really very complicated or not feasible. The hardest part is keeping up with all of the changing technology. It seems that many times you just learned something and you have to learn the new version all over again."

proves to employers that you have reached a high level of knowledge in the field.

Earnings

Entry-level computer network specialists earn about $42,800 to $59,800 per year to start, according to Robert Half International. Mid-range salaries for those with several years of experience and further training are generally around $65,000. The highest salaries in this field are around $80,000. These salaries are earned by those with experience, additional training, and willingness to learn.

Outlook

Employment for computer network specialists is expected to grow faster than average through 2008, according to the U.S. Department of Labor. Network administrators are in high demand, particularly those with Internet experience.

FOR MORE INFO

Contact ACM for information on internships, student membership, and the ACM student magazine, Crossroads. ACM also offers a student Web site at http://www.acm.org/ membership/student/.
Association for Computing Machinery
1515 Broadway
New York, NY 10036-5701
212-869-7440
http://www.acm.org

For information on certification and education, contact:
Network Professional Association
195 C Street, Suite 250
Tustin, CA 92780
714-573-4780
http://www.npa.org

For information on scholarships, student membership, and the student newsletter, looking.forward, contact:
IEEE Computer Society
1730 Massachusetts Avenue, NW
Washington, DC 20036
202-371-0101
http://www.computer.org

Computer Operators

When mathematician Grace Hopper (1906-1992) was young, her hobbies were needlepoint, reading, and playing the piano. Her father encouraged her to pursue things that interested her, even if they were considered more "masculine" pursuits. In 1943, she was sworn into the U.S. Navy Reserve and served for 43 years.

Hopper coined the term "bug," meaning a computer fault, while working on the Harvard Mark I computer. The real bug in the Mark I was a moth that caused a hardware problem.

In 1969 the Data Processing Management Association named her the first computer science "Man of the Year," and she was awarded the National Medal of Technology in 1991.

What Computer Operators Do

Computer operators, sometimes called *data entry clerks,* prepare information to be entered into a computer and then type it in. They read information from checks, bills, and other forms and enter it into the computer using a regular keyboard or numbers only keypad. They check the accuracy of their work regularly.

Computer programmers develop the operating instructions for a particular computer system, and computer operators follow these instructions. Their tasks may also include setting controls on the computer, loading tapes, disks, and paper, and watching the screen for any messages or abnormalities. Some computer operators prepare printouts for all the people in a company who will be using the computer. They keep logbooks or records noting each job that runs and any malfunctions that occur during their shifts.

As computers become more and more sophisticated, computer operators have to keep up with new technologies. Some companies now have computers that can perform some of an operator's easier tasks automatically, such as scanning information, which allows some operators to take on more challenging responsibilities. These responsibilities include investigating and reporting complicated mistakes or glitches that occur in the system to appropriate supervisors. Most jobs for computer operators are in companies, industries, or organizations that process a large amount of information. These include banks, insurance companies, government agencies, accounting firms, utilities, and other industries.

Education and Training

Most people working as computer operators in large companies are high school graduates. Some have college or technical school education. Large companies look for applicants who have fast and accurate typing skills. They also prefer applicants who are familiar with computers and several software programs. In smaller companies, requirements for entry-level jobs as computer operators are the same, but might also include typical secretarial skills. Most companies pro-

EXPLORING

• Learn as many software programs as you can, including database, spreadsheet, and word processing programs. Join computer clubs sponsored by your school or community.

• Volunteer your computer operating skills at local charities or community centers. They need people to keep accurate records and maintain data for their organizations.

RELATED JOBS

Computer and Electronics Sales Representatives

Computer and Office Machine Technicians

Electronics Engineering Technicians

Electronics Service Technicians

vide on-the-job training courses lasting several days or weeks.

Earnings

According to the U.S. Department of Labor, median annual earnings of computer operators were about $25,000 in 1998. Salaries can range from $16,260 to $39,130. In the federal government, computer operators with a high school diploma started at about $21,600 a year in 1999. Those with one year of college started at $23,000.

Median annual earnings for computer operators were $24,300 in computer and data processing services, $23,600 in hospitals, $22,600 in personnel supply services, $22,500 in the federal government, and $20,200 in commercial banks. According to Robert Half International, the average starting salaries for console operators ranged from $26,000 to $35,500 in 1999.

Outlook

The use of computers has grown tremendously in the past few years, but this growth is expected to decline sharply through 2008. Opportunities will be best for operators who are familiar with a variety of operating systems and who

ALPHABET SOUP

ASCII: American Standard Code for Information Interchange
ANSI: American National Standard Institute
BPS: Bits Per Second
CPU: Central Processing Unit
DPI: Dots Per Inch
FTP: File Transfer Protocol
GUI: Graphical User Interface
HDD: Hard Disk Drive
HTTP: HyperText Transmission Protocol
ISP: Internet Service Provider
LAN: Local Area Network
NQS: Network Queuing System
RAM: Random Access Memory
ROM: Read Only Memory
URL: Uniform Resource Locator
WAN: Wide Area Network

keep up to date with the latest technology.

Improvements in data-processing technology enable businesses to process greater volumes of information with fewer workers, so the employment outlook for data entry clerks is expected to show little change or grow more slowly than average through 2008. Jobs are becoming limited, for example, because many computer systems can now send information directly to another computer

FOR MORE INFO

Contact ACM for information on internships, student membership, and the ACM student magazine, Crossroads. ACM also offers a student Web site at http://www.acm.org/ membership/student/.
Association for Computing Machinery
1515 Broadway
New York, NY 10036-5701
212-869-7440
http://www.acm.org

system without the need for a data entry clerk to input the information a second time.

There were about 251,000 computer operators employed in 1998. Most jobs are found in wholesale trade companies, manufacturing companies, data processing services, financial institutions, and government agencies that have data processing needs.

Computer Trivia

• The late John Tukey, professor of statistics at Princeton, coined the terms "software" and "bit."

• The first hard drive available for the Apple had a capacity of 5 megabytes.

• The average mousepad is eight and three quarters by seven and a half inches.

• In many cases, the amount of storage space on a recordable CD is measured in minutes. 74 minutes is about 650 megabytes, 63 minutes is 550 megabytes.

Computer Programmers

What Computer Programmers Do

Computer programmers write and code the instructions for computers. Computer programmers work for companies that create and sell computer hardware and software. They also work for all kinds of businesses, from manufacturers of office machines to distributors of machinery and equipment. They work for banks, hospitals, schools, and the federal government.

Programmers break down each step of a task into a series of instructions that the computer can understand. Then programmers translate the instructions into a specific computer language. COBOL and FORTRAN are examples of two computer languages. Then programmers test the program to make sure it works. They correct any errors. This is called debugging the program. Finally, they write the instructions for the operators who will use the program. Some programs can be created in a few hours. Others may take more than a year of work. Programmers often work together on teams for a large project.

There are two basic kinds of computer programmers: *systems programmers* and *applications programmers.* Systems programmers must understand and care for an entire computer system, including its software, its memory, and all of its related equipment, such as terminals, printers, and disk drives. Systems programmers often help applications programmers with complicated tasks. Applications programmers write the programs that do particular tasks—word processing, accounting, databases, and games. They usually specialize in a field, such as business, engineering, or science.

One example of a programming specialty is numerical tool programming. *Numerical control tool programmers,* or *computer numerical control (CNC) programmers,* write programs that direct machine tools to perform their functions automatically. CNC programmers must understand how various machine tools operate and also know the properties of the metals and plastics that are used in the process. In direct numerical control, several

EXPLORING

• The best way to learn about computers is to use one—either at home surfing the Internet or at school.

• Join a computer club and find others who are interested in computers and programming.

• It is a good idea to start early and get some hands-on experience operating and programming a computer.

• You will find countless books on programming at your local library or bookstore. There are plenty of resources to teach yourself no matter how much experience you have.

RELATED JOBS

Computer Security Specialists
Computer Systems Analysts
Database Specialists
Graphics Programmers
Software Designers

COMPUTERS ARRIVE ON THE SCENE

Data processing systems developed during World War II. The amount of information that had to be collected and organized for war efforts became so great that it was not possible for people to prepare it in time to make decisions. A quicker way had to be invented.

After the war, the new computer technology was put to use in other government operations as well as in businesses. The first computer used by civilians was installed by the Bureau of the Census in 1951 to help gather data from the 1950 census. At this time, computers were large, cumbersome, and energy-draining. Three years later, the first computer was installed by a business firm. Today, computers are used in government agencies, industrial firms, banks, insurance agencies, schools, publishing companies, scientific laboratories, and homes.

machines are controlled by a central computer.

Education and Training

Most employers prefer to hire college graduates. There are many colleges that offer courses and degree programs in computer science. A number of two-year programs in data processing, and junior-level programming are available in junior and community colleges. Some employers may want their programmers to be trained in their specific area. For example, a computer programmer for an engineering firm might need an engineering degree. Most employers look for candidates who are patient, persistent, very logical in their thinking, and who can work under pressure without making mistakes.

Because programmers work in so many different industries, there is no standard way to begin as a computer programmer. After you learn the basics of computer programming, you should choose a field that interests you and then look for programming opportunities in that field. It can take up to a year to master all aspects of a programming job. Opportunities for advancement are great.

Earnings

The average earnings for full-time programmers were about $45,550 a year in 1998, according to U.S. Department of Labor figures. Salaries can range from $27, 800 to $88,700 a year. Jobs in the West and Northeast pay more than those in the South and Midwest.

Outlook

According to the U.S. Department of Labor, employment opportunities for computer programmers will grow faster than average through 2008. The best jobs will go to college graduates who know several programming languages, espe-

FOR MORE INFO

For more information, contact the following organizations:
Association for Computing Machinery
One Astor Plaza
1515 Broadway
New York, NY 10036
212-869-7440
http://www.acm.org

Association of Information Technology Professionals
315 South Northwest Highway, Suite 200
Park Ridge, IL 60068-4278
800-224-9371
http://www.aitp.org

cially newer ones used for computer networking and database management. The best jobs will also go to those who have some training or experience in an applied field such as accounting, science, engineering, or management.

Computer Security Specialists

Computer Security in the Movies

War Games (1983)
Matthew Broderick plays a teenage computer guru who cracks into a government defense system and nearly starts another world war.

Sneakers (1992)
A high-tech team of security experts, led by Robert Redford, steals a black box that contains super secret security information.

The Net (1995)
Sandra Bullock's identity is messed with when some computer data she has is wanted by someone else.

Hackers (1995)
Fisher Stevens is a hacker with a criminal mind and tries to frame a group of computer whizzes for his crimes. The whiz kids then use their hacking skills to prove their innocence.

What Computer Security Specialists Do

A *computer security specialist* is responsible for protecting a company's network from intrusion by outsiders. These intruders are called hackers (or crackers), and the process of breaking into a system is called hacking (or cracking). Computer security specialists are sometimes known as *Internet security specialists, Internet security administrators, Internet security engineers, information security technicians,* or *network security consultants.* A computer security specialist may work as a consultant—someone brought in from outside the company to work on a project—or as an in-house employee—someone who works full-time for that company.

When a company connects to the Internet, computer security specialists set up systems known as firewalls. Firewalls act as barriers of protection between the outside world of the Internet and the company by limiting access or permitting access to users.

In-house computer security specialists are in charge of watching the flow of information through the firewall. They must be able to write code and configure the software to alert them when certain kinds of activities occur. They monitor all access to the network and watch for anything out of the ordinary. If they see something strange, they investigate and sometimes track down the user who initiated the unusual action. Specialists may create a new program to prevent that action from happening again.

Computer security specialists may also be in charge of virus protection. Viruses are programs written to purposely harm a hard drive and can enter a network through email attachments or infected floppy disks. Specialists may create the security policies for the company and educate employees on those policies.

Computer security specialists who work as consultants design and implement solutions for a company's security problems. They must understand the needs of the company, determine if there are inse-

EXPLORING

• Check out programming books from the local library and learn how to write simple code.
• School science clubs and competitions offer opportunities to experiment with computer programming. They also encourage you to work with other students and get experience working in teams.
• Surf the Web and research the many security issues that face users today. Check the various information security Web sites and organizations that deal with Internet security. Use a search engine and the keywords "Internet AND Security" or "Network AND Security" or "Information AND Security."
• National news magazines, newspapers, and trade magazines are great sources of information on current trends and hiring practices.

HACKERS AND THEIR ALIASES

Captain Crunch—John Draper was perhaps the first "phreak." In the 1970s, he discovered that a toy whistle he found in a box of Cap'n Crunch cereal had the same frequency as a Wide Area Telephone System line. He used it to make unlimited, free phone calls until he was caught.

Condor—Kevin Mitnik is possibly the most renowned hacker. In 1994-95 he successfully broke into all kinds of sites including military sites, financial institutions, and software and technology companies.

Agent Steal—Justin Tanner Peterson was at one time an FBI informant and ratted out Kevin Mitnik and others. Prior to that, he cracked a consumer credit agency.

Phiber Optic, Acid Phreak, and **Scorpion**—These three worked together until they were caught in 1990 with thousands of passwords and credit card numbers on disk.

Analyzer—This 18-year-old Israeli cracked into the United States government computers. He was arrested in March of 1998.

curities within the company's network, and find ways to correct them.

Education and Training

Take as many computer science and programming classes as possible to prepare for this career. Spend time in the school computer lab, learn how computers work, and play with the latest technologies. Many colleges offer computer science, networking, and programming degrees, which are highly recommended. Most computer degrees also require studies in mathematics.

Earnings

The field of Internet security is a high-paying career and the salary potential is growing. The low end of the pay scale is $25,000 a year and is probably what you would make in an entry-level position at a small company. The majority of computer security specialists make between $50,000 and $75,000 a year. If you have a lot of experience and an excellent reputation in the industry, you can earn as much as $120,000 a year.

Outlook

Employment for computer security specialists will grow much faster than the average through 2008. The number of companies with Web sites is exploding. As these companies connect their private networks to the Internet, they will need to protect their confidential information. Currently, the demand for Internet security specialists is greater than the supply, and this trend is expected to continue.

FOR MORE INFO

CERT Coordination Center
Software Engineering Institute
Carnegie Mellon University
Pittsburgh, PA 15213-3890
412-268-7090
http://www.cert.org

This professional organization for information security professionals provides education and training for its members.
Computer Security Institute
600 Harrison Street
San Francisco, CA 94107
415-905-2626
http://www.gocsi.com

In addition to providing security products and services, ICSA has a professional membership organization and also runs groups that share research and information on current security issues.
International Computer Security Association
12012379-C Sunrise Valley Drive
Reston, VA 20191-3422
703-453-0500
http://www.icsa.net/

Information Security Magazine is published by ICSA for the information security professional.
Information Security Magazine
Information Security
106 Access Road
Norwood, MA 02062
781-255-0200
http://www.infosecuritymag.com/

Computer Systems Analysts

Where Do They Work?

Computer systems analysts work for all types of firms, like these:

Manufacturing companies

Data processing service firms

Hardware and software companies

Banks

Insurance companies

Credit companies

Publishing companies

Government agencies

Colleges and universities

What Computer Systems Analysts Do

Computer systems analysts help banks, government offices, and businesses understand their computer systems. Most offices now use computers to store data. They need analysts who can design computer systems and programs for the specific needs of a business, or even to the needs of just one department in a business.

Computer systems analysts work with both the hardware and software parts of computer systems. Hardware includes the large items such as the computer itself, the monitor, and the keyboard. Software includes the computer programs, which are written and stored on disks, and the documentation (the manuals or guidebooks) that goes with the programs. Analysts design the best mix of hardware and software for the needs of the company that employs them.

A computer systems analyst for the personnel department of a large company, for example, would first talk to the department manager about which areas of the business could be helped by computer technology. If the company started a new policy of giving employees longer paid vacations at Christmas, the manager might want to know how this policy has affected company profits for the month of December. The analyst can show the manager what computer program to use, what data to enter, and how to read the charts or graphs that the computer produces. The work of the analyst allows the manager to review the raw data. In this case, the numbers show that company profits were the same as in the previous Decembers. The manager can then decide whether to continue the company policy.

Once analysts have the computer system set up and operating, they advise on equipment and programming changes. Often, two or more people in a department each have their own computer, but they must be able to connect with and use information from each other's computers. Analysts must then work with all the different computers in a department or a company so the computers can connect with each other. This system of connected computers is called a network.

EXPLORING

• Play strategy games, such as chess. Such games are a good way to use analytic thinking skills while having fun. Commercial games range in themes from war simulations to world historical development.

• Learn everything you can about computers. Work and play with them on a daily basis. Surf the Internet regularly and read computer magazines. You might want to try hooking up a mini-system at home or school, configuring terminals, printers, and modems. This activity requires a fair amount of knowledge and should be supervised by a professional.

Education and Training

To be a computer systems analyst you will need at least a bachelor's degree in computer science. Analysts in specialized areas (aeronautics, for example) usually have graduate degrees as well. Also, training in mathematics, engineering, accounting, or business will be helpful in some cases.

In addition to a college degree, job experience as a computer programmer is very helpful. Many businesses choose computer programmers already on staff and train them on the job to be systems analysts.

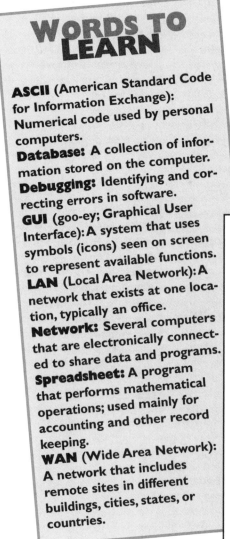

WORDS TO LEARN

ASCII (American Standard Code for Information Exchange): Numerical code used by personal computers.

Database: A collection of information stored on the computer.

Debugging: Identifying and correcting errors in software.

GUI (goo-ey; Graphical User Interface): A system that uses symbols (icons) seen on screen to represent available functions.

LAN (Local Area Network): A network that exists at one location, typically an office.

Network: Several computers that are electronically connected to share data and programs.

Spreadsheet: A program that performs mathematical operations; used mainly for accounting and other record keeping.

WAN (Wide Area Network): A network that includes remote sites in different buildings, cities, states, or countries.

Salaries in Information Technology

The following is a list of staff positions in the thriving IT industry and the corresponding entry-level salaries:

Senior Systems Analyst	$49,488
Senior Systems Programmer	$48,445
Systems Analyst/Administrator	$44,507
Information Security Specialist	$44,439
E-Commerce Network Administrator	$42,571
Systems Programmer	$41,332
Network Administrator	$41,036

From ComputerWorld's 14th annual salary survey, September 2000

Computer systems analysts with several years of experience are often promoted into managerial jobs.

Although it is not required, computer systems analysts can become certified by the Institute for Certification of Computer Professionals. Analysts take classes and exams to become a Certified Systems Professional (CSP). This certification may help you get a job.

Earnings

Starting salaries for computer systems analysts average about $46,300 a year. After several years of experience, analysts can earn as much as $59,000 a year. Computer systems analysts with many years of experience and a master's degree can earn salaries of $63,000 a year and higher. Salaries for analysts in government are somewhat lower than the average for private industry. Earnings also depend on years of experience

FOR MORE INFO

For more information about the career of computer system analyst, contact the following organizations:

Association for Systems Management
1433 West Bagley Road
PO Box 38370
Cleveland, OH 44138
216-234-2930

Institute for Certification of Computing Professionals
2200 East Devon Avenue, Suite 246
Des Plaines, IL 60018
800-843-8422
http://www.iccp.org

and the type of business you work for.

Outlook

This field is one of the fastest growing careers through 2008. Companies are always looking for qualified analysts, especially those with advanced degrees in computer science.

Computer Trainers

What Computer Trainers Do

Today's employees and students need to know how to send email, how to use the Internet, and how to use word processing programs. However, many people become frustrated when faced with a blank computer screen and a thick instruction manual. Sometimes, too, the computers and programs are too complex to be explained fully and clearly by a manual. *Computer trainers* teach people how to use computers, software, and other new technology. When a business installs new hardware and software, computer trainers work one-on-one with the employees, or they lead group training sessions. They may also offer instruction over the Internet. With technology changing every day, computer trainers are called upon often for support and instruction.

Computer trainers teach people how to use computer programs. For example a company's accounting department may

Carnegie-Mellon University

Computer trainers must know their subject backwards and forwards in order to answer questions from both beginning and advanced students.

need a computer trainer to teach its accounting clerks how to use a spreadsheet program, which is used to make graphs and charts, and to calculate sums. Other common business programs include database programs, which keep track of such things as customer names, addresses, and phone numbers, and word processing programs, which are used to create documents, letters, and reports. Some computer trainers may also teach computer programming languages such as C or Visual Basic.

Many corporations, advertisers, and individuals have set up home pages on the Internet. A computer trainer can help them use the language needed to design a page, and teach them how to update the page. Trainers teach people how to operate desktop publishing programs and laser printers that allow individuals and

EXPLORING

• Use your library, bookstores, and the Internet to keep up with the latest software and technology. The Internet has thousands of sites on computers and computer training.

• Teach yourself as many software packages as you can.

• Teach new programs to your parents, grandparents, or younger sisters and brothers.

THE HISTORY OF COMPUTING ON THE WEB

IEEE Computer Society History of Computing
http://www.computer.org/50

The Virtual Museum of Computing
http://www.comlab.ox.ac.uk/archive/other/museums/computing.html

Past Notable Women of Computing
http://www.cs.yale.edu/homes/tap/past-women-cs.html

businesses to create interesting graphics and full-color pages for brochures and newsletters. Some computer trainers may also help offices set up their own office network. With a network, all the computers in an office can be linked. Employees then share programs and files, conference with other employees, and send electronic mail.

Computer trainers may be self-employed and work on a freelance basis, or they may work for a computer training school or computer service company.

Education and Training

Most community colleges, universities, and vocational schools offer computer courses. Computer service companies and training schools also offer courses in specific software programs. Though college courses and training are important, it helps to have experience, too. You can get experience by working with computers on a regular basis, either at home or in the work place. Computer experience can also come from working in the sales department of a computer store or software company.

Education requirements vary at computer training schools and computer service companies. To work as a teacher in a high school or community college, a bachelor's degree is the minimum requirement.

Earnings

The average training specialist earns about $40,500. Senior training specialists average $47,400 a year, and training managers earn about $57,000. In general, salaries for computer trainers increase with the level of education.

Computer trainers often earn yearly bonuses. In 1996, bonuses for training specialists averaged $1,600, senior training specialists received $2,500, and training managers were awarded $5,200 on average.

Outlook

The outlook for computer trainers is excellent through 2008

FOR MORE INFO

The American Society for Training and Development
1640 King Street, Box 1443
Alexandria, VA 22313-2043
http://www.astd.org

International Association of Information Technology Trainers
PMB 4516030-M Marshalee Drive
Elkridge, MD 21075-5935
410-290-7000
http://www.itrain.org

because more people are using computers than ever before.

Information from the EQW National Employer Survey says that more employers are using a variety of outside training providers. According to the American Society of Training and Development, the short life cycles of technology products, combined with the greater complexity of many job roles, will increase the demand for computer trainers.

Database Specialists

What Database Specialists Do

The collection of information stored in a computer by business, industry, and the government is called a database. *Database specialists* work for utility companies, stores, investment companies, insurance companies, publishing firms, telecommunications firms, and for all branches of government. They set up and maintain databases. They purchase computer equipment and create computer programs that collect, analyze, store, and send information.

Some database specialists figure out the type of computer system their company needs. They meet with top-level company officials to discuss these needs. Together they decide what type of hardware and software will be required to set up a certain type of database. Then a *database design analyst* writes a proposal that states the company's needs, the type of

IBM

A database manager uses recent publications to update a computer file used by clients for information services.

equipment that will meet those needs, and how much the equipment will cost.

Database specialists set up the computer system that the company buys. Database managers and administrators decide how to organize and store the information in the database. They create a computer program or a series of programs and train employees to enter information into computers.

Computer programs sometimes crash, or work improperly. Database specialists make sure that a backup copy of the program and the database is available in case of a crash. Specialists also are

EXPLORING

• School computer clubs offer a good way to learn about computers and meet others interested in the field.
• There are training programs, such as those offered at summer camps and community centers, that teach computer literacy.
• Volunteer to work on databases at your school, religious institution, or local charity.

responsible for protecting the database from people or organizations who are not supposed to see it. A company's database contains important, and sometimes secret, information.

Very large companies may have many databases. Sometimes it is necessary for these databases to share information. Database managers see to it that these different databases can communicate with each other, even if they are located in different parts of the country.

Education and Training

If you are interested in becoming a database specialist, you should take as many computer courses as possible. In addition, you should study mathematics, accounting, science, English, and communications. An associate's degree in a computer-related technology is required for entry-level database administrators. You need a bachelor's degree in computer science or business administration for advanced positions. Those with a master's degree will have even greater opportunities.

Earnings

Beginning database design analysts with a college education earn about $35,000 per year. Mid-level salaries, offered to professionals with several years of expe-

FYI

The IT industry has suffered from a critical shortage of skilled workers. One solution to this employment problem may lie in the hiring of people with mental disabilities. Those with neurological disorders such as autism have been excelling at IT work in data entry, programming, and Web design. IT projects require the talents possessed by many workers with mental disabilities: creativity, problem-solving abilities, and great concentration. The computer also gives these workers structure and allows them to somewhat avoid the prejudices against mental disabilities.

rience, average about $50,000. After even more experience and further training, database design analysts are offered top salaries of over $70,000. According to the U.S. Department of Labor, database specialists earned an average of $47,900 in 1998. Salaries ranged from $26,700 to $86,200. Database administrators and consultants working for major computer companies usually earn higher salaries.

Outlook

The use of computers and database systems in almost all business creates good opportunities for well-qualified database personnel. Database specialists and computer support specialists are predicted by the U.S. Department of Labor to be the two fastest growing occupations through 2008. Those with the best education and the most experience in computer systems and personnel management will find the best job prospects.

For More Info

Institute for Certification of Computing Professionals
2200 East Devon Avenue, Suite 247
Des Plaines, IL 60018
http://www.iccp.org

Association of Information Technology Professionals
315 South Northwest Highway, Suite 200
Park Ridge, IL 60068-4278
800-224-9371
http://www.aitp.org

Related Jobs

Computer Network Administrators
Computer Programmers
Computer Systems/Programmer Analysts
Computer Trainers
Database Design Analysts
Internet Security Specialists
Software Designers
Systems Set Up Specialists
Technical Support Specialists

Desktop Publishing Specialists

The Desktop Publisher's Idea Book: One-of-a-Kind Projects, Expert Tips, and Hard-to-Find Sources by Chuck Green (Random House, 1997).

Desktop Publishing and Design for Dummies by Roger C. Parker (IDG Books Worldwide, 1995).

How to Make Money Publishing from Home: Everything You Need to Know to Successfully Publish: Books, Newsletters, Greeting Cards, Zines, and Software by Lisa Angowski Rogak Shaw. (Prima Publishing, 1997).

How to Start a Home-Based Desktop Publishing Business by Louise M. Kursmark (Globe Pequot, 1996).

What Desktop Publishing Specialists Do

If you have made flyers to advertise a music recital or printed up programs for a school play, then you have probably worked with computers, desktop publishing software, and printers. *Desktop publishing specialists* do this for a living. They create reports, brochures, books, business cards, and other documents. They work with files others have created, or they compose original text and graphics for their clients. Desktop publishing specialists have graphic design skills, proofreading skills, and a knowledge of illustration and page layout software. They also have sales and marketing abilities.

Individuals and small business owners hire desktop publishing specialists to create printed documents and Internet Web pages. Programs such as *FreeHand*, *Illustrator*, *PhotoShop*, *Quark Express*, and *PageMaker* are popular desktop publishing programs. Desktop publishing specialists create interesting graphics, arrange the text on the page, select font types and sizes, arrange column widths, and check for proper spacing between letters, words, and columns. Proofreading is also important. They check for spelling and typing errors. Desktop publishing specialists prepare documents for printing, so they also handle issues such as resolution for graphhics and photos, pagination, registration, and color specification.

Desktop publishing specialists work closely with their clients, making sure to create the documents according to specifications. After creating the file and getting final approval from clients, they either give the files on disk to the customer or, in some cases, they give files to the printer and manage the project through the printing process.

Education and Training

Desktop publishing specialists need a good eye for detail in addition to computer and artistic skills. Start taking computer classes that teach both hardware and software. Photography classes can teach you about color, composition, and design. Art classes will help you learn graphic design skills, while English classes help

EXPLORING

• Work on your school paper and yearbook to get experience with page layout, typesetting, word processing, and how to meet deadlines.

• Experiment with your home computer, or a computer at school or the library. Play around with various graphic design and page layout programs.

• If you subscribe to an Internet service, take advantage of any free Web space available to you and design your own home page.

• Join computer clubs and volunteer at small organizations to produce newsletters and flyers.

you learn about editing and composition.

A degree is not required to become a desktop publishing specialist, but it may be helpful to earn a two-year associate's degree in graphic design, commercial art, or advertising.

Earnings

Entry-level desktop publishing specialists with little or no experience generally earn minimum wage. Electronic page makeup system operators earn an average of $14 to $17 an hour, and scanner operators earn from $15 to $18 an hour.

According to the U.S. Department of Labor, full-time *prepress workers* in typesetting and composition earn a median wage of $443 a week, or about $23,000 annually. Wages vary depending on experience, training, region, and size of the company. According to a salary survey conducted by the Printing

WORDS TO LEARN

Bleed: An element that extends to the edge of a page.

Body copy: The main text in a publicaton.

Copyfitting: Forcing text to fit a space by editing copy, changing the spacing between letters or lines of type, or adjusting type size.

Flip: To change an item so that it appears as a mirror image of the original.

Leading: The space between lines of text.

Pica: A measurement used in printing. There are 6 picas to an inch.

Point: A unit of typographic measurement. A point is 1/72 of an inch, and there are 12 points in one pica.

Registration: The alignment of overlaying pieces.

Resolution: Sharpness of detail. Usually measured in dots per inch.

Industries of America in 1997, desktop publishing specialists made anywhere from $12 an hour to $40 an hour.

Outlook

According to the U.S. Department of Labor, the field of desktop publishing will be one of the fastest growing occupations, increasing about 75 percent through 2008. In 1998, there were a total of 26,000 desktop publishing specialists employed in the United States.

Desktop publishing specialists will benefit from faster, easier publishing programs as computer technology continues to advance. Traditional typesetting by a printer costs over $20 a page, while desktop printing can cost less than a penny a page. With speedier, more cost efficient ways to create documents, businesses will use more desktop publishing services.

FOR MORE INFO

For more information on scholarships and education, contact:
Association for Suppliers of Printing and Publishing Technologies
1899 Preston White Drive
Reston, VA 20191-4367
703-264-7200
http://www.npes.org

For scholarship information, contact:
National Scholarship Trust Fund of the Graphic Arts
200 Deer Run Road
Sewickley, PA 15143
http://www.gatf.org

To receive an issue of Desktop Publishers Journal, *contact:*
Desktop Publishers Journal
462 Boston Street
Topfield, MA 01983
http://www.dtpjournal.com

For career brochures and information about grants and scholarships, contact:
Society for Technical Communication
901 North Stuart Street, Suite 904
Arlington, VA 22203-1822
703-522-4114
http://www.stc-va.org

Graphics Programmers

What Graphics Programmers Do

To perform properly, a computer must be told what to do, how to do it, and when to do it. These sets of instructions are called computer programs. Programmers design software that allows the computer to perform many different tasks. *Graphics programmers* write software programs that enable the computer to produce designs and illustrations that help business, industry, and schools. Programmers use special computer languages, such as **Visual BASIC** and **C++**, to write their programs.

Graphics programmers write the code that produces two- and three-dimensional illustrations with color, lighting, shading, morphing, animation, and special effects. They create new programs for medical imaging devices; geological research; virtual testing systems for aircrafts, cars, and spacecraft; and special effects and animation for Hollywood productions.

Graphics programmers have expertise in mathematics, particularly geometry and algorithms. (An algorithm is a step-by-step procedure for solving a problem.) They first look at what the final graphics should look like. For example, a medical school might want a computer program that shows various views of different parts of the body. The program might show the skeletal system, muscles, organs, and vascular system. Each part of the body might need to be viewed from the front, side, and back, as well as in a cross section.

Graphics programmers create a flowchart to show the order in which a computer will process information to produce each view of each body part. They write code in a computer language that tells the computer mathematically how to draw the graphics. Graphics programming is a long process. Once the initial program is completed, it goes through testing, rewriting code, and debugging until it is ready to be used.

Education and Training

To become a graphics programmer, you must earn a college degree in computer science. To prepare for college, take courses in computer science, English,

EXPLORING

• **Work on your school newspaper or yearbook to get experience with graphics and illustration programs.**

• **Join a computer club, especially one that has other members interested in programming.**

• **Start learning programming languages, such as Visual BASIC and C++.**

RELATED JOBS

Computer Programmers
Computer Systems Analysts
Computer-Aided Design
Database Design Analysts
Drafters
Graphic Designers
Software Engineers

mathematics, science, and foreign languages. Art or graphic design courses will help you develop a good sense of composition, proportion, perspective, and other elements of art.

In college, you should complete a general computer science program. Courses should include computer graphics but not be limited to graphics only. There is much competition for

EXPLORING PROGRAMMING LANGUAGES

Programming languages tell computers how to work. Programmers for the first comuters wrote instructions in machine language, which consisted of binary digits (series of 1s and 0s) that represented operation codes and memory addresses. Since this system is difficult to use, assembly languages were invented. These enabled programmers to write instructions in alphabetic symbols (such as AD for add and SUB for subtract) rather than in numbers.

FORTRAN (acronym for Formula Translation) was invented in 1956. FORTRAN was well suited to scientists and mathematicians because it was similar to mathematical notations.

A more practical programming language, COBOL (Common Business-Oriented Language) was invented several years later. COBOL uses words and syntax resembling those of ordinary English.

BASIC (Beginner's All-Purpose Symbolic Instruction Code) is used in schools, businesses, and homes for microcomputer programming.

C is a language that is used in a lot of commercial software.

PASCAL (named for the French scientist-philosopher Blaise Pascal) is widely used for microcomputers.

Fourth-generation languages (4GLs) are used mostly for database management or as query languages. Examples of these include FOCUS, SQL (Structured Query Language), and dBASE.

C++ and Smalltalk are used to write programs incorporating self-contained collections of data structure or computational instructions, called "objects."

computer programming jobs, so you might want to consider earning a graduate degree.

Earnings

Beginning graphics programmers earn between $35,000 and $45,000 a year. More experienced programmers or those with more education can earn between $50,000 and $57,000 a year. Programmers who work as independent consultants can earn more than $68,000 a year, but their salaries may not be regular. Overall, those who work for industry earn the most.

Outlook

The demand for all types of computer programmers is strong, and employment is expected to grow much faster than the average for all occupations through 2008. This is especially true for graphics programmers. The number of openings exceeds the number of qualified graphics programmers. One specialty expected to grow is CAD/CAM technology, which will need twice the number of programmers it now employs.

FOR MORE INFO

For more information, contact the following organizations:
Association for Computing Machinery
Special Interest Group on Computer Graphics
11 West 42nd Street
New York, NY 10036
212-869-7440
http://www.siggraph.org

For information on scholarship, student membership, and the student newsletter, looking.forward, contact:
IEEE Computer Society
1730 Massachusetts Avenue, NW
Washington, DC 20036-1992
202-371-0101
http://www.computer.org

Hardware Engineers

Read All About It

Charles Babbage and the Engines of Perfection by Bruce Collins and James MacLachlan (Oxford University Press, 2000).

The Computer Hardware Industry: The WetFeet.com Insider Guide by WetFeet.com, Gary Alpert, and Steve Pollock (WetFeet Press, 1999).

How Computers Work: Millennium Edition by Ron White (Que, 1999).

Principles of Computer Hardware by Alan Clements (Oxford University Press, 2000).

The Universal History of Computing: From the Abacus to the Quantum Computer by Georges Ifrah (John Wiley & Sons, 2000).

What Hardware Engineers Do

Computer *hardware engineers* work with the insides of a computer, including motherboards, memory chips, CPUs, hard drives, floppy drives, CD-ROM drives, removable storage, video cards, sound cards, network cards, and modems. They improve, repair, and change parts to keep up with the demand for faster and stronger computers and better software programs.

Some hardware engineers specialize in the design of computers or microprocessors. Others specialize in designing and organizing information systems for business and the government. They may also work with peripheral devices, such as printers, scanners, keyboards, speakers, and monitors.

The first step for most hardware projects is to describe the new device and its function. Will it be a tiny electronic component such as a transistor? Will it be part of a huge industrial robot? Or will it be a microprocessor or other specialized board? Once they define the function, engineers design the actual component and make plans for its assembly.

Engineers need to consider the device's overall effectiveness and reliability, its cost, and safety. Once the device is made, it is tested and evaluated, several times if necessary. Sometimes engineers also design the machinery that will manufacture the device.

Tools such as Computer Aided Design (CAD) help engineers create three-dimensional designs that are easily manipulated by a computer. Hardware engineers also use different network systems such as Local Area Networks (LAN) and Wide Area Networks (WAN), among others, as well as specific programming languages suited to their companies' needs. Many engineers work as part of a team of specialists who use science, math, and electronics to improve existing technology or create new solutions.

Education and Training

You can get a head start on your computer career by taking computer, electronics,

EXPLORING

• Join a computer club with others who are interested in hardware. You may find a mentor who can teach you about hardware components.

• Find someone who would be willing to give you old computers that they are going to throw away. Use the parts to reconstruct a new computer or fix one that needs repair. Examine various parts and see if you can tell how they are made.

RELATED JOBS

Computer Programmers
Computer Systems Analysts
Microelectronics Technicians
Semiconductor Technicians
Software Engineers
Systems Set Up Specialists
Technical Support Specialists

and programming classes now. Being able to communicate effectively with co-workers and clients is important, so prepare yourself by taking speech and writing courses.

Most computer professionals have a bachelor's degree in computer science or engineering. Another choice is to earn a two-year degree or certification in a computer-related specialty. Many employers, though, prefer to hire and advance those with a bachelor's or advanced degree in computer science.

Beginnings

Early forerunners of the computer were the abacus, developed in ancient times in the Far East, and an adding machine invented in 1641 by Blaise Pascal of France. The principle of using a punched card to encode information was developed about 1801 by Joseph Marie Jacquard, also of France. His cards were used to control the pattern produced in textiles by a loom.

All of the basic parts of the modern digital computer—input and output devices, storage and arithmetic units, and the sequencing of instructions—were conceived in the 1820s and 1830s by Charles Babbage, an English mathematician. He completed a small computer, called a difference engine, in 1822. It consisted primarily of gears and levers and was similar to a modern mechanical desk calculator.

Earnings

According to a 1998 National Association of Colleges and Employers salary survey, hardware design and development engineers (with a computer science degree) earn average starting salaries of $43,300. Graduates with an engineering background earn average salaries between $35,700 and $40,700. Graduates of master's programs in computer engineering earn average starting salaries of about $50,650.

Outlook

Computer engineering will be one of the three fastest growing occupations through the year 2008, according to the U.S. Department of Labor. Tremendous growth is the result of factors such as greater business use of the Internet, networking of information and resources within companies, and technical advancements. A college education will help you secure a promising future in this industry.

FOR MORE INFO

To find out more about a career as a hardware engineer, contact:
Association for Computing Machinery
1515 Broadway, 17th Floor
New York, NY 10036-5701
http://www.acm.org

For employment information, links to online career sites for computer professionals, and background on the industry, contact:
Institute of Electrical and Electronics Engineers
3 Park Avenue, 17th Floor
New York, NY 10016-5997
http://www.ieee.org

For information on a career in computer engineering, computer scholarships, or a copy of Computer Magazine, contact:
IEEE Computer Society
1730 Massachusetts Avenue, NW
Washington, DC 20036-1992
202-371-0101
http://www.computer.org

For certification information, contact:
Institute for Certification of Computing Professionals
2200 East Devon Avenue, Suite 247
Des Plaines, IL 60018-4503
http://www.iccp.org

Internet Content Developers

How It All Began

The Internet developed from ARPANET, an experimental computer network established in the 1960s by the U.S. Department of Defense. By the late 1980s the Internet was being used by many government and educational institutions. In the early 1990s, public use of the Internet increased dramatically, spurred by the development of the Web.

The Web had its beginnings in 1991, when hypertext code was developed, primarily as a means of creating links between scholarly articles on the Internet. In 1993 the first Web browser, Mosaic, became available, developed by programmers at the University of Illinois. Mosaic added graphic capabilities to the existing system of links. Businesses quickly realized the commercial potential of the Web and soon developed their own Web sites. By early 1998, the number of Web sites on the Internet had grown to 2,000,000.

What Internet Content Developers Do

Internet content developers are sometimes called *Web developers* or *Web designers.* They create Internet sites for small businesses, large corporations, and Internet consulting firms.

Internet content developers design Web sites and sometimes write the code that runs and navigates it. Internet developers know Internet programming languages such as Perl, Visual BASIC, CGI, Java, ActiveX, C++, and HTML. Developers also know the latest graphic file formats and other Web production tools.

Content developers work with companies to decide what to include or not include on their Web sites and how to present it. They consider goals for the Web site—some companies use the Internet simply to describe their identity, while others sell merchandise or information, present news and commentary, provide entertainment, or offer a forum for exchange of ideas, to name a few possibilities.

Content developers also consider the potential users of the site. They try to design features that are original, that will attract attention, and be easy to navigate. A Web site can include hundreds of elements, such as text, photographs, artwork, video clips, audio clips, bulletin boards, order forms, search features, links to related Web sites, advertising banners, and animated text and graphics.

Part of the content development process involves designing a general layout for the site and all its connected pages. Text is written and edited and artwork and photos are scanned. All of the elements are then converted into the proper code so that they can be placed on the server.

Education and Training

If you are interested in this career, take as many courses as possible in computer science, science, and mathematics. These classes will give you a good foundation in computer basics and problem-solving skills. English and speech classes will improve your communication skills.

EXPLORING

• Read national news magazines, newspapers, and trade magazines or surf the Web for information about Internet careers. You can also visit a variety of Web sites to study what makes them appealing or not so appealing.
• If your school has a Web site, get involved in the planning and creation of new content for it. If not, talk to your computer teachers about creating one, or create your own site at home.
• Here are some reading suggestions:
Build Your Own Website by Robert L. Perry (Franklin Watts, Inc., 2000).
Creating and Publishing Web Pages on the Internet by Art Wolinsky (Enslow Publishers, Inc., 1999).
Make Your Own Web Page! A Guide for Kids by Ted Pedersen, et al (Price Stern Sloan Publishing, 1998).

THE INTERNET EXPLOSION

In the summer of 2000, Internet experts estimate more than 300 million people worldwide were using the Internet on a frequent basis for business, research, shopping, personal correspondence, social interactions, entertainment, listening to radio, and sharing information.

Five years from now, some predict that there will be more than one billion users worldwide with more than 700 million users living outside of North America. Now, a little more than half of the Internet users speak English as their primary language. It is predicted that English-speakers will continue to dominate the Internet for a few more years to come, but there is an increasing number of non-English Web sites and more sites hosted outside English-speaking countries.

Source: United States Internet Council

You will need a bachelor's degree in computer science or computer programming, although some developers earn degrees in noncomputer areas, such as marketing, graphic design, or information systems. Whatever degree you earn, you should have an understanding of computers and computer networks and knowledge of Internet programming languages. Further training and hands-on experience is available through internships or entry-level positions. One year of experience working on a site is a great help toward landing a job in the field.

Earnings

An entry-level position in Web development at a small company pays around $30,000. As you gain experience or move to a larger company, you might make $50,000. The top of the pay scale is around $74,000 per year. Differences in pay tend to follow the differences found in other careers: companies in the Northeast pay more than those in the Midwest or South, and men are paid more than women. According to a 1998 survey of its members by the Association of Internet Professionals, the average salary of content developers was $50,986.

Outlook

The career of Internet content developer, like the Internet itself, is growing much faster than the average. As more companies look to go worldwide, they need developers who have the ability and expertise to create the sites to bring their products, services, and corporate images to the public and to other businesses. Content developers can expect Internet technology to continue to develop at a fast pace.

For More Info

For information on scholarships, student membership, and the student newsletter, looking.forward, contact:
IEEE Computer Society
1730 Massachusetts Avenue, NW
Washington, DC 20036-1992
202-371-0101
http://www.computer.org

AIP represents the worldwide community of people employed in Internet-related fields.
Association of Internet Professionals
9200 Sunset Boulevard, Suite 710
Los Angeles, CA 90069
800-JOIN-AIP
http://www.association.org/index.html

Related Jobs

Desktop Publishing Specialists
Graphic Designers
Internet Security Specialists
Technical Writers and Editors
Webmasters

Microelectronics Technicians

Where Microchips Are Used

Radar

Microwave technology

Radio

Television

Computers

Calculators

X rays

Stereos

Compact disc players

Robotics

Space technology

Weapons systems

What Microelectronics Technicians Do

Microelectronics technicians work in research laboratories helping develop and construct custom-designed microchips. Microchips, often called simply "chips," are tiny but extremely complex electronic devices that control the operations of many kinds of communications equipment, consumer products, industrial controls, aerospace guidance systems, and medical electronics. The process of manufacturing chips is called fabrication.

Microelectronics technicians usually work from a schematic prepared by an engineer. The schematic contains a list of the parts needed to construct the component and the layout that the technician will follow. The technician gathers the parts and prepares the materials to be used. Following the schematic, the technician constructs the component and then uses a variety of sophisticated, highly sensitive equipment to test the component's performance.

If the component doesn't work, microelectronics technicians troubleshoot the design, trying to find where the component has failed, and replace one part for a new or different part. Test results are reported to the engineering staff, and the technician may help evaluate the results and prepare reports.

After the testing period, the microelectronics technician often assists in the technical writing of the component's specifications. These specifications are used for integrating the component into new or redesigned products or for developing a process for the component's large-scale manufacture.

Education and Training

Classes in algebra, geometry, chemistry, and physics will prepare you for a postsecondary educational program or apprenticeship. Industrial classes, such as metalworking, wood shop, auto shop, and machine shop, and similar courses in plastics, electronics, and construction techniques are helpful.

EXPLORING

• Join science, computer, or electronics clubs.

• Work on electronics projects at home. You can find many resources for electronics experiments and projects in your school or local library or on the Internet.

RELATED JOBS

Electrical and Electronics Engineers
Electronics Engineering Technicians
Electronics Service Technicians
Graphics Programmers
Hardware Engineers
Semiconductor Technicians

Postsecondary school education or training is a requirement for entering the field. Two-year training programs in electronics are offered at community college or vocational training facilities where you can earn a certificate or an associate's degree. There are also three- and four-year apprenticeship programs that include on-the-job training with an employer.

Earnings

Lane Community College in Oregon advises its microelectronics students that they can expect entry-level salaries of between $18,000 and $25,000 a year. According to Wageweb.com, salaries for electronics technicians in 2000 ranged from a minimum average of $19,805 to an average of $25,300, and a maximum of $30,920.

Microelectronics technicians earn average salaries of

WORDS TO LEARN

Capacitor: An element in an electrical circuit used to store a charge temporarily.
Conductor: A substance that conducts an electrical charge.
Insulator: A material that does not conduct electricity.
Integrated circuit: A tiny chip of material imprinted or etched with many interconnected electronic components.
Microchip, or chip: A tiny slice of semiconducting material processed to hold specific electrical properties in order to be developed into an integrated circuit. Also refers to an integrated circuit.
Resistor: A device that provides resistance, used to control electric current.
Schematic: A diagram that provides structural and/or procedural information on the construction of an electrical or mechanical system.
Semiconductor: The basic component of microchips. A solid, crystalline substance (especially silicon in electronics) with conducting properties between true conductors and insulators.
Transistor: A small, electronic device used in a circuit as a switch, detector, or an amplifier.

$28,000, according to the U.S. Department of Labor. Those in managerial or supervisory positions earn higher salaries, ranging between $33,000 and $50,000 a year.

Outlook

Jobs in the electronics industry are expected to grow faster than the average through 2008, according to the U.S. Department of Labor. This is because of increasing competition within the industry and the rapid technological advances in the electronics industry. Electronics is also a rapidly growing industry, and the use of electronic technology will become more and more important to every aspect of people's lives. This in turn will create a demand for workers with skills and training.

FOR MORE INFO

For information on certification, contact:
International Society of Certified Electronics Technicians
2708 West Berry Street
Fort Worth, TX 76109-2356
817-921-9101
http://www.iscet.org/

For employment information, links to online career sites for computer professionals, and background on the industry, contact:
Institute of Electrical and Electronics Engineers
3 Park Avenue, 17th Floor
New York, NY 10016-5997
http://www.ieee.org

FYI

According to the Semiconductor Industry Association, annual industry sales of chips exceeded $200 billion for the first time in 2000. The industry has grown 17 percent over the past 40 years. Much of this growth is because of the demand for data networking, broadband, wireless, optoelectronics, and personal computers. SIA expects the industry to grow to $319 billion by 2003.

Software Designers

What Is Software?

The term "software" was coined to differentiate it from "hardware," which is the physical parts of the computer system. A set of instructions that directs a computer's hardware to perform a task is called a program, or software program.

There are three types of software. *System software* controls a computer's internal functioning, usually through an operating system, and runs such extras as monitors, printers, and storage devices. *Application software* directs the computer to carry out commands given by the user. Application software includes word processing, spreadsheet, database management, inventory, and payroll programs. *Network software* coordinates communication between the computers that are linked in a network.

What Software Designers Do

Without software, computers would not be able to work. Computers need to be told exactly what to do. Software is the set of codes that tells a computer what to do. It comes in the form of the familiar packaged software that you find in a computer store, such as games, word processing programs, spreadsheets, and desktop publishing programs. Software also comes in special forms designed for the specific needs of a particular business. *Software designers* create these software programs, also called applications. *Computer programmers* then create the software by writing the code that gives the computer instructions.

Software designers must imagine every detail of what a software application will do, how it will do it, and how it will look on the screen. An example is how a home accounting program is created. The software designer first decides what the program should be able to do, such as balance a checkbook, keep track of incoming and outgoing bills, and keep records of expenses. For each of these tasks, the software designer decides what menus and icons to use, what each screen will look like, and whether there will be help or dialog boxes to assist the user. For example, the designer may want the expense record part of the program to produce a pie chart that shows the percentage of each household expense in the overall household budget. The designer can ask that the program automatically display the pie chart each time a budget is completed or only after the user clicks on a special icon on the toolbar.

Some software companies build custom-designed software for the specific needs or problems of one business. Some businesses are large enough that they employ in-house software designers who create software applications for their computer systems.

Education and Training

Computer, science, and math classes will prepare you for a career as a software designer. In high school, you should take as many computer, science, and math courses as possible. English and speech

EXPLORING

• **Learn as much as you can about computers.**

• **Keep up with new technology by reading computer magazines and by talking to other computer users.**

• **Join computer clubs.**

• **Use online services and the Internet for information about this field.**

• **Advanced students can put their design/ programming knowledge to work by designing and programming their own applications, such as simple games and utility programs.**

LIFE AS A SOFTWARE CONSULTANT

antrix Software Group Inc., in Chicago, Illinois, creates custom software applications using Microsoft tools. David Carpenter, president and founder, has been developing software since 1984. Before he started Cantrix in 1992, he held senior technical positions for companies such as AT&T and Motorola.

Carpenter has a bachelor's degree in computer science and engineering from the University of Illinois. He has taught Visual BASIC and advanced C++ programming languages. He is also proficient in several other computer languages, including SQL, Ada, and C.

Carpenter says, "People who want to succeed in this field need to be focused, analytical, creative, and adaptable. If you are an independent learner, buy a PC and start teaching yourself a language like Microsoft Visual BASIC. There are many resources on the World Wide Web to help you get started.

"Also, take the time in school to learn the craft of high-quality, well-designed software development, as opposed to the ad hoc, quick development that is so prevalent in the industry. It will pay high rewards."

classes help improve communication skills, which are important to software designers who make formal presentations to their managers and clients.

To be a software designer, you will need a bachelor's degree in computer science plus at least one year of experience with a programming language.

You also need knowledge of the field that you will be designing software for, such as education, business, or science. For example, someone with a bachelor's degree in computer science with a minor in business or accounting has an excellent chance for employment in creating business and accounting software.

Earnings

Salaries for software designers vary with the size of the company and with location. Software designers' salaries range from $50,000 a year as a beginning designer to $65,000 a year. Senior designers or project team leaders can earn $80,000 a year. Software design managers' salaries can reach $100,000 a year or more.

Outlook

Jobs in software design are expected to grow faster than the average through 2008, according to the U.S. Department of Labor. Employment of computing professionals is expected to increase as technology advances. The expanding use of the Internet by businesses has caused a growing need for skilled professionals.

FOR MORE INFO

Contact ACM for information on internships, student membership, and the ACM student magazine, Crossroads. *ACM also has a student Web site at http://www.acm.org/membership/student/*
Association for Computing Machinery
1515 Broadway
New York, NY 10036-5701
212-869-7440
http://www.acm.org

For information on scholarships, student membership, and the student newsletter, looking.forward, *contact:*
IEEE Computer Society
1730 Massachusetts Avenue, NW
Washington, DC 20036
202-371-0101
http://www.computer.org

RELATED JOBS

Computer and Video Game Designers
Computer Programmers
Database Specialists
Software Engineers

Software Engineers

Most software engineers are employed by computer and data processing companies and by consulting firms. Software engineers also work in:

Medicine

Industry

Military

Communications

Aerospace

Science

What Software Engineers Do

Businesses use computers to do complicated work for them. In many cases, their needs are so specialized that commercial software programs cannot perform the desired tasks. *Software engineers* change existing software or create new software to solve problems in many fields, including business, medicine, law, communications, aerospace, and science. For example, many software engineers are now working on projects to automate government and business forms. In the near future, it will be possible for almost everyone to fill out tax returns, insurance claims, and many other forms directly on the computer.

The projects software engineers work on are all different, but their methods for solving a problem are similar. First, engineers talk to clients to find out their needs and to define the problems they are having. Next, the engineers look at

Since computers only do exactly what they are told, software engineers have to write a programming command for every bit of information.

IBM

the software already used by the client to see whether it could be changed or if an entirely new system is needed. When they have all the facts, software engineers use scientific methods and mathematical models to figure out possible solutions to the problems. Then they choose the best solution and prepare a written proposal for managers and other engineers.

Once a proposal is accepted, software engineers and technicians check with hardware engineers to make sure computers are powerful enough to run the new programs. The software engineers then outline program details. *Engineering technicians* write the initial version in computer languages.

EXPLORING

• Learn as much as you can about computers and computer software. Read computer magazines and talk to other computer users.

• Join computer clubs and surf the Internet for information about working in this field.

Throughout the programming process, engineers and technicians run diagnostic tests on the program to make sure it is working well at every stage. They also meet regularly with the client to make sure they are meeting their goals and to learn about any changes the client wants.

When a software project is complete, the engineer prepares a demonstration of it for the client. Software engineers might also install the program, train users, and make arrangements to help with any problems that arise in the future.

Education and Training

It is strongly recommended that you at least earn an associate's degree in computer technology. With an associate's degree, you can find a software engineering technician position. A bachelor's degree is required for most software engineers.

Another choice besides formal education at a technical/vocational school or university is commercial certification. Several large computer companies sponsor training and certification exams in many computing fields.

ADVICE FROM A PRO

On the Web site, JobProfiles.com, software engineer Bruce says education is key. "To program you must have an ability to group your thoughts into a logical pattern. But you have to learn the language you wish to code in and this takes time. Never give up. Start with the simple problems and move on up to the more complex ones. Find a good software company that is willing to take on individuals who are willing to be persistent in solving the problems. You won't always succeed, but keep at it. In time it will start making sense and then the fun really begins. . . . There is a certain thrill in solving a problem with code and even more when one can go back later and see a faster way of doing it."

Source: http://www.jobprofiles.com

Earnings

Software engineering technicians usually earn beginning salaries of $24,000 a year. Computer engineers with a bachelor's degree in computer engineering earn starting salaries of $45,700 a year in 1999, according to the National Association of Colleges and Employers. New computer engineers with a master's degree earn $58,700. Experienced software engineers can earn more than $100,000 a year. Software engineers generally earn more in areas where there are lots of computer companies, such as the Silicon Valley in northern California.

Outlook

Software engineering is one of the fastest growing occupations through 2008. Computer companies, consulting firms, major corporations, insurance agencies, banks, and other industries hire software engineers.

FOR MORE INFO

For more information, contact the following organizations:

Software & Information Industry Association
1730 M Street, NW, Suite 700
Washington, DC 20036-4510
202-452-1600
http://www.siia.net

Institute for Certification of Computing Professionals
2200 East Devon Avenue, Suite 247
Des Plaines, IL 60018
847-299-4227
http://www.iccp.org

Contact ACM for information on internships, student membership, and the ACM student magazine, Crossroads.
Association for Computing Machinery
1515 Broadway
New York, NY 10036-5701
212-869-7440
http://www.acm.org

RELATED JOBS

Computer Network Specialists
Computer Programmers
Database Specialists
Webmasters

Technical Support Specialists

What Technical Support Specialists Do

Technical support specialists investigate and solve computer problems. They listen to customer complaints, discuss possible solutions, and write technical reports.

Technical support can be divided into two areas—user support and technical support. *User support specialists* answer calls from users who have problems with their computers. They listen carefully as the user explains the problem and the commands entered that seemed to cause the problem. They then try to work with the user to resolve the problem. If the problem is user error, the support specialist explains the mistake and teaches the correct procedure. If the problem is in the hardware or software, the specialist isolates the problem and recommends a solution. The support specialist may have to consult supervisors or programmers.

IBM

A technical support specialist tries to solve a customer's software problem.

EXPLORING

• **Start working and playing on computers as much as possible. Many computer professionals became computer hobbyists at a very young age. Surf the Internet, read computer magazines, and join school or community computer clubs.**

• **Look for special computer classes and demonstrations in your area.**

• **Learn as many software programs as you can. Also learn about networks, hardware, and peripheral equipment.**

Technical support specialists solve problems with a computer's operating system, hardware, or software. They use resources, such as engineers or technical manuals, to get more information. They may modify or re-install software programs or replace hardware parts. Technical support specialists who work in large corporations oversee the daily operations of the various computer systems in the company, determine if upgrades are needed, and work with other computer experts to modify commercial software to the company's specific needs. Technical support specialists who work for hardware and software manufacturers solve problems over the phone or Internet, or they may visit a client's site. They answer questions about installation, operation, and customizing.

Education and Training

You need a high school diploma to become a technical support specialist. More advanced training is not a standard requirement for this job because technology changes too quickly to be taught in a formal education program. An associate's degree in a computer-related subject can show potential employers that you are proficient in general computer technology.

Earnings

Technical support specialists earned a median of about $37,100 in 1998, according to the U.S. Department of Labor.

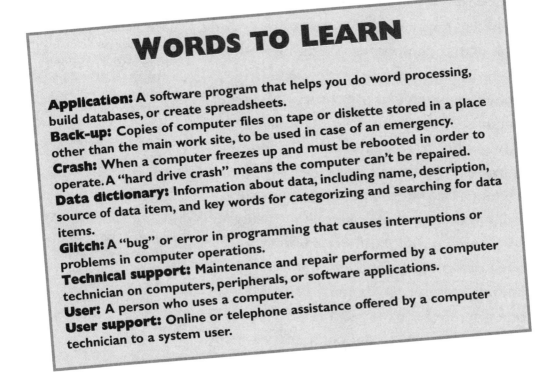

WORDS TO LEARN

Application: A software program that helps you do word processing, build databases, or create spreadsheets.

Back-up: Copies of computer files on tape or diskette stored in a place other than the main work site, to be used in case of an emergency.

Crash: When a computer freezes up and must be rebooted in order to operate. A "hard drive crash" means the computer can't be repaired.

Data dictionary: Information about data, including name, description, source of data item, and key words for categorizing and searching for data items.

Glitch: A "bug" or error in programming that causes interruptions or problems in computer operations.

Technical support: Maintenance and repair performed by a computer technician on computers, peripherals, or software applications.

User: A person who uses a computer.

User support: Online or telephone assistance offered by a computer technician to a system user.

Salaries ranged from $22,900 to more than $73,800. Technical support specialists earned the following median annual salaries in 1997 by industry: management and public relations, $37,900; computer and office equipment, $36,300; computer and data processing services, $36,300; professional and commercial equipment, $35,700; and personnel supply services, $35,200.

Outlook

The U.S. Department of Labor predicts that technical support specialists will be one of the fastest growing of all occupations through the year 2008. It forecasts huge growth—about 100 percent—of additional support jobs through the year 2008. Technical support specialist jobs are especially plentiful in northern California and Seattle, Washington.

Every time a new computer product is released on the market or another system is installed, there will unavoidably

FOR MORE INFO

For more information about jobs in technical support, contact:

Association for Computing Machinery
1515 Broadway
New York, NY 10036
212-869-7440
http://info.acm.org/

IEEE Computer Society
1730 Massachusetts Avenue, NW
Washington, DC 20036-1992
202-371-0101
http://computer.org

be problems, whether from user error or technical difficulty. Therefore, there will always be a need for technical support specialists to solve the problems. Since technology changes so rapidly, it is very important for support specialists to keep up-to-date on advances.

Webmasters

The Internet developed from ARPANET, an experimental computer network established in the 1960s by the U.S. Department of Defense. By the late 1980s, the Internet was being used by many government and educational institutions. In the early 1990s public use of the Internet increased dramatically, spurred by the development of the Web.

The Web had its beginnings in 1991, when hypertext code was developed. In 1993, the first Web browser, Mosaic, became available, developed by programmers at the University of Illinois. Businesses quickly realized the commercial potential of the Web and soon developed their own Web sites. By early 1998, the number of Web sites on the Internet had grown to 2,000,000. Researchers at the Online Computer Library Center claim that the Web now contains 7,128,000 unique sites.

What Webmasters Do

Webmasters create and manage Web sites for large corporations, small businesses, nonprofit organizations, government agencies, schools, special interest groups, and individuals.

Some webmasters develop the content for the pages they manage. They may write the text or receive it from other writers and editors. Webmasters insert codes into the text in HyperText Markup Language (HTML). HTML codes tell the computer how to arrange and format the text. Webmasters also select images and scan them into the document. Images are also coded with HTML to put them in the desired size and position.

Many Web sites contain information that changes regularly. An organization may make changes once a month. A newspaper may post updates several times in one day. Webmasters maintain and update Web sites, inserting current data.

Web sites usually have links to other pages or other Web sites. Webmasters check the links and make sure visitors to the site can connect easily to the information they need.

Webmasters also keep track of activity to the site. They note how often people visit their site. They answer questions and comments from visitors, usually by email. Some webmasters are in charge of processing customer orders for products or services.

Education and Training

Many webmasters have bachelor's degrees in liberal arts, engineering, or computer science. Others have two-year degrees from a technical or vocational school.

Most people who enter the field, however, do have a background of work experience in computer technology. When considering candidates for the position of webmaster, employers usually require at least two years' experience with various Web technologies, including knowledge of HTML, JavaScript, and SQL. It is quite common for someone to move into the position of webmaster from another com-

EXPLORING

• Spend time surfing the Web. Look at a variety of Web sites to see how they look and operate.

• Design your own personal Web page. Many Internet providers offer their users the option of designing and maintaining a personal Web page for a very low fee. A personal page can contain virtually anything that you want to include—snapshots of friends, audio files of favorite music, or links to other favorite sites.

puter-related job in the same organization.

Earnings

According to *U.S. News & World Report,* salaries for the position of webmaster range from $50,000 to $100,000 a year. The demand for webmasters is so great that some companies are offering stock options, sign-on bonuses and other benefits, in addition to salaries from $80,000 to $110,000. Many webmasters, however, move into their positions from another position within their company or perform webmaster duties in addition to other duties. These employees tend to receive lower salaries.

According to the 1998 Webmaster Survey by Collaborative Marketing, the majority of webmasters earn under $50,000. Nineteen percent of all webmasters earned from $25,000 to $40,999 annually and 17 percent earned less than $25,000. Salary.com reports that the median base salary for webmasters is $52,272 a year.

Outlook

The World Organization of Webmasters projects an explosion of jobs available through the year 2008—well over 8 million. The majority of webmasters working today are full-time employees—about 86 percent according to the 1998 Webmaster Study, conducted by Collaborative Marketing. This study also showed that 35 percent of webmasters are between the ages of 26 and 35. Companies are eager to fill webmaster positions with computer-savvy young people.

FOR MORE INFO

For information on schools that offer webmaster training, webmaster specialties, and a certification program, contact:
International Webmasters Association
119 East Union Street, Suite #E
Pasadena, CA 91103
626-449-3709
http://www.iwanet.org

For education and certification information, contact:
World Organization of Webmasters
9580 Oak Avenue Parkway, Suite 7-177
Folsom, CA 95630
916-929-6557
http://www.world-webmasters.org/

RELATED JOBS

Computer Programmers
Desktop Publishing Specialists
Graphic Designers
Internet Content Developers
Internet Security Specialists
Technical Support Specialists
Technical Writers and Editors

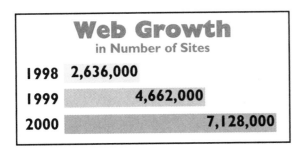

Web Growth
in Number of Sites

1998	2,636,000
1999	4,662,000
2000	7,128,000

Glossary

accredited: Approved as meeting established standards for providing good training and education. This approval is usually given by an independent organization of professionals to a school or a program in a school. Compare **certified** and **licensed**.

apprentice: A person who is learning a trade by working under the supervision of a skilled worker. Apprentices often receive classroom instruction in addition to their supervised practical experience.

apprenticeship: 1. A program for training apprentices (see apprentice). 2. The period of time when a person is an apprentice. In highly skilled trades, apprenticeships may last three or four years.

associate's degree: An academic rank or title granted by a community or junior college or similar institution to graduates of a two-year program of education beyond high school.

bachelor's degree: An academic rank or title given to a person who has completed a four-year program of study at a college or university. Also called an undergraduate degree or baccalaureate.

certified: Approved as meeting established requirements for skill, knowledge, and experience in a particular field. People are certified by the organization of professionals in their field. Compare **accredited** and **licensed**.

community college: A public two-year college, attended by students who do not live at the college. Graduates of a community college receive an associate degree and may transfer to a four-year college or university to complete a bachelor's degree. Compare **junior college** and **technical college**.

diploma: A certificate or document given by a school to show that a person has completed a course or has graduated from the school.

doctorate: An academic rank or title (the highest) granted by a graduate school to a person who has completed a two- to three-year program after having received a master's degree.

fringe benefit: A payment or benefit to an employee in addition to regular wages or salary. Examples of fringe benefits include a pension, a paid vacation, and health or life insurance.

graduate school: A school that people may attend after they have received their bachelor's degree. People who complete an educational program at a graduate school earn a master's degree or a doctorate.

intern: An advanced student (usually one with at least some college training) in a professional field who is employed in a job that is intended to provide supervised practical experience for the student.

internship: 1. The position or job of an intern (see intern). 2. The period of time when a person is an intern.

junior college: A two-year college that offers courses like those in the first half of a four-year college program. Graduates of a junior college usually receive an associate degree and may transfer to a four-year college or university to complete a bachelor's degree. Compare **community college.**

liberal arts: The subjects covered by college courses that develop broad general knowledge rather than specific occupational skills. The liberal arts are often considered to include philosophy, literature and the arts, history, language, and some courses in the social sciences and natural sciences.

licensed: Having formal permission from the proper authority to carry out an activity that would be illegal without that permission. For example, a person may be licensed to practice medicine or to drive a car. Compare **certified**.

major: (in college) The academic field in which a student specializes and receives a degree.

master's degree: An academic rank or title granted by a graduate school to a person who has completed a one- or two-year program after having received a bachelor's degree.

pension: An amount of money paid regularly by an employer to a former employee after he or she retires from working.

private: 1. Not owned or controlled by the government (such as private industry or a private employment agency). 2. Intended only for a particular person or group; not open to all (such as a private road or a private club).

public: 1. Provided or operated by the government (such as a public library). 2. Open and available to everyone (such as a public meeting).

regulatory: Having to do with the rules and laws for carrying out an activity. A regulatory agency, for example, is a government organization that sets up required procedures for how certain things should be done.

scholarship: A gift of money to a student to help the student pay for further education.

social studies: Courses of study (such as civics, geography, and history) that deal with how human societies work.

starting salary: Salary paid to a newly hired employee. The starting salary is usually a smaller amount than is paid to a more experienced worker.

technical college: A private or public college offering two- or four-year programs in technical subjects. Technical colleges offer courses in both general and technical subjects and award associate degrees and bachelor's degrees.

technician: A worker with specialized practical training in a mechanical or scientific subject who works under the supervision of scientists, engineers, or other professionals. Technicians typically receive two years of college-level education after high school.

technologist: A worker in a mechanical or scientific field with more training than a technician. Technologists typically must have between two and four years of college-level education after high school.

undergraduate: A student at a college or university who has not yet received a degree.

undergraduate degree: See **bachelor's degree**.

union: An organization whose members are workers in a particular industry or company. The union works to gain better wages, benefits, and working conditions for its members. Also called a labor union or trade union.

vocational school: A public or private school that offers training in one or more skills or trades. Compare **technical college**.

wage: Money that is paid in return for work done, especially money paid on the basis of the number of hours or days worked.

Index of Job Titles

Computers
on the Web

Ainsworth Computer Seminar
http://www.qwerty.com/startacs.htm

Click-N-Learn
http://www.kids-online.net/learn/c_n_l.html

Internet for Kids
http://kidsinternet.about.com/kids/kidsinternet/

KidsWeb Computers
http://www.kidsvista.com/sciences/computers.html/

spaceCAD
http://library.thinkquest.org/C006970F

UCS: The Ultimate Computer Source
http://library.thinkquest.org/25018

Youth Tech
http://www.youthtech.com/linkus.htm